MY GOALS
AKA
MISSION STATEMENT:

www.ingramcontent.com/pod-product-compliance
Lightning Source LLC
Chambersburg PA
CBHW070234220526
45465CB00004B/1420
9798615498510